THE EMPLOYER BRAND HANDBOOK

Volume 1:
The Real World Guide
to Working With Recruiters

James Ellis

Saltlab

ISBN: 9798642596203

First Printing, 2020

Printed by Amazon, United States

Saltlab
Attn: James Ellis
421 W Melrose
Chicago, IL 60657

saltlab.com

Cover and book design by: James Ellis

CONTENTS

"Too many people believe the future is something that happens and just rolls them over in its wake."
-Cindy Gallop

"Inspiration is for amateurs;
the rest of us just show up and get to work."
- Chuck Close

READER'S GUIDE:
WHY READ THIS BOOK

I've written this part of the book two other times so I'm giving up. I'll just say it straight: Employer brand, for better or worse, is often tied to recruiting. Most companies see employer brand as a means to solve the problem "how do I get more people to apply?" rather than problems like, "how can I get more people to fall in love with our company?" or "how can I get all elements inside and outside the company to align to a common purpose, a common 'why?'"

I get it. In the Maslov's mythical hierarchy of employer brand needs, filling the top of the funnel usually comes first. Increasing retention and understanding talent targets comes later.

But you can't just magically make pipelines shift, especially when there's an existing function there ostensibly dedicated to supporting that pipeline: recruiting.

Recruiters own the pipeline. They own the candidate. In many companies, they can have their own individual processes. Aside from their own salaries, the company has invested in an expensive ATS, some sourcing tools, maybe a LinkedIn recruiter seat and expect them to bring in enough candidates to hit their hiring targets.

And here you come, trying to shake things up with your cool "employer brand way of thinking."

It's no surprise that new and even experienced employer brand practitioners see the recruiting team both as the most important relationship to build, but also as the hardest nut to crack. Recruiters have lived in their own world for a very long time. Even if they are using the latest tools, chances are, they are working on a playbook written before you were born. It may not make sense to you, but that's just how they are.

Now, that's not to denigrate recruiters. They have an insanely hard job. They step up and get rejected (sometimes rudely) dozens of times a day. They are trying to serve two masters: the candidate and the hiring manager. Every single one has a horror story about how much time and effort they put into a candidate, how they dragged that candidate through the interview process, prepped them for the big interview, negotiated salary and bonus and all sorts of other details, only to have the candidate walk away at the last minute. Or worse, accept the offer only to announce that they would be taking a different role the day before their start date.

Like I said, it's a rough gig. So it stands to reason that they get to set some of the ground rules.

But therein lies the challenge. If you can learn their rules, their customs, their strange way of doing things, you can teach them some new tricks (though, at the beginning, it will feel more like they are teaching you some things). And if you teach them enough tricks, you'll find that they are aligned to your brand and brand strategy. They will become soldiers in your volunteer army to make the company better.

And that will make you far more effective at your own job. (See? I got your back.)

Here's the secret: you can't look good until you make them look good. Got it? Good.

So this book is for you, the person who owns the employer brand but has no idea how to get recruiters to help out. Rather than talk strategy, this is a workbook, complete with guides, checklists, and examples of exactly what to say and how to say it.

The book is broken up into projects that should be started in order. Skipping a project may seem like no big deal, but you might realize how future projects depended on its being there. It might make sense to read the whole book (c'mon, it's not that big) so you can see how all the elements come together and support each other over time.

The Employer Brand Handbook

A DOWN AND DIRTY INTRO
TO EMPLOYER BRANDING

I am emotionally and contractually obligated to define employer branding. Why? I'm talking to employer brand professionals, am I not? Why should I define what we all already understand, if not to pad the word count?

Truely, I am not yet willing to bet that more than 50% of the people who read this have a common usable definition in mind. I've talked to so many people who still see employer branding as "recruitment marketing with a pedigree" or "inbound recruiting." And while, if you squint just right, is those things, it's a lot more. A lot more.

So here's my working definition: Employer brand is the aggregated perceptions and feelings of all individuals about what they think it must be like to work at your company, based on all related experiences, information and touchpoints.

Why is this important? Well first, we need to remember that strong employer branding isn't just in any one aspect of the company. It isn't limited to the ratings site or the career site. It is every interaction a person has with the brand, whether they are looking for a job currently or not. That means that when scandals, product announcements, awards, layoffs, COVID-19 responses, reviews, word of mouth, and about a thousand other things impact the employer brand.

But you probably don't have any authority over all those things. In fact, you probably don't have authority over any of those things. And yet you are expected to own the brand. This is why your job is so much fun (and by "fun," I mean exciting, interested, and fraught with uncertainty at every conceivable level).

You might ask yourself why this ends up being your job. I mean, aren't things like job postings and recruiter content things that recruiters are tasked with?

Let me put it this way: If you want to positively influence your employer brand, you have a few thousand levers you can attempt to pull. Some are easy and some are hard. Some are useful so only vaguely so. And since you have a finite amount of resources and time, you need to be smart about which levers you focus on.

Which is why focusing on the recruiting and TA team is crucial. These teams oversee a huge swath of those touchpoints. If you build strong relationships with recruiters, if you can get them to adjust their thinking and even some actions, you will see remarkable changes in your brand for almost no cost.

For example, let's say one recruiter with access to a LinkedIn recruiter seat spam-InMails 100 nurses in your area about a job, but in a pushy way. Those nurses don't respond positively to that kind of approach and ignore the email. The problem is that nurses talk to nurses and one bad InMail may change the perception by the local nurses community on what your brand is about. And since those 100 nurses now have a negative impression of your brand, what happens when a great recruiter reaches out with a truly great opportunity? That negative brand impression will change the likelihood of that great hire from even reading the message because of the lingering taste your first recruiter left.

So yes, recruiting plays a huge role in your ability to get things done. Which is why you need to get serious about recruiters. Which is why you're here.

The Employer Brand Handbook

EXPLAINING EMPLOYER BRANDING
TO SKEPTICS

As much as I love metaphors and abstraction, getting someone, even a recruiter, to understand the value of employer branding to their ability to attract and hire talent, requires a stark example.

On one hand, I hold the job posting for a project manager. On the other hand, I hold another job posting for a project manager. One of these postings is from a massively successful software company. Another posting is from a company that manufactures ceramics and toilets.

The thing is, without the brand at the top, the job postings are almost identical. It is very possible that both were pulled from the same book of job descriptions. Without the brand, you can't tell if you're applying for a wild and crazy, fast-paced software company or a staid and stable manufacturing company. And if the candidate can't tell the difference, you have to ask, "why is the candidate applying at all?"

9

If you want to get more of the right kind of people to see your logo on a job board or in an InMail message and think, "Wow! I would love to work for them!" you need to plant that seed of an idea that yours is a cool company well before that interaction occurs.

You need to get recruiters to see employer brand as an asset that they can leverage to attract more of the right people to apply to their jobs. The brand sets you apart and makes it crystal clear why a candidate might fall in love with you and choose you. Once that idea is obvious, recruiters will have better (more authentic, more credible, more attractive) messaging, a more aligned candidate experience, and more success recruiting, even as the talent market remains stiff.

And if that doesn't work, let them know you appreciate their skepticism, but hope they have an open mind as they see how strong employer branding helps recruiters who do embrace it.

CONTENT STRATEGY FILLS THE FUNNEL

I'm a content marketer at heart. It's how I got my start in digital marketing, so the ideas of sharing stories and other things of value to develop a relationship you'll tap into later, is very closely aligned to how great employer branders think. Which is why so much of the work you'll do with and for recruiters is focused on content strategy.

Recruiters do a very one-to-one job. They talk to candidates, facilitate conversations, liaise with hiring managers and interview loops, follow-up and debrief, and even sometimes negotiate the final offer, all of which is a very retail approach to work. This means that there's almost nothing stopping the recruiter from saying whatever it takes to keep the candidate hooked, whether it is true or… a deep aspiration.

I'm not saying recruiters lie. I'm saying they are incentivized to close the deal however they can.

You get to take a different approach because rather than see things at "ground level," you have a different perspective. You don't live or die by every rejected offer. You see a slightly bigger picture. And you can see that recruiter one might be spinning tails to keep the fish on the hook, but when the fish askes around, all those amazing claims made by the recruiter seem paper-deep. And the candidate walks away.

But what if you reveal and clarify a common brand, build content that you scatter all around the web that aligns to that brand, and provide all the validation a candidate needs to see that the recruiter claims are credible. Suddenly, recruiters don't need to spin such tall tails to keep the candidate interested.

And that's your content strategy: build stories and content around the brand, make them as closely tied to teams, roles and offices to provide concreteness, and allow the candidate to find these stories all around the web like so many scattered leaves. This allows the candidate to create their own picture of what it's like to work there, one that is influenced if not outright shaped by you, because you made that story obvious and real.

That's our strategy when it comes to leveraging recruiters: have them share stories we make, have them tell stories that align, and use those stories to build relationships and attract candidates so something real about the company.

PROJECTS AND GUIDES

Personally, I love (love!) nerding out on the theory and strategy around employer brand, possibly to the point where having talked about branding for hours, I may never say "here's how to actually make that happen."

So I built this book out as a series of projects you can walk through. This isn't a comprehensive list of ways to help recruiters, but if you knock most of these out in the right way, if you use them as ways to build deep relationships with recruiters over time, you'll almost certainly come up with your own ideas on how to keep the relationship growing. So once you get these done, don't think you're done. Instead see these as ways to train recruiters on employer branding and prove to recruiters you can help them do a better job and find their own success.

MAPPING THE HIRING PROCESS

I might be cynical (and black-hearted and a little evil), but recruiting processes all too often feel like they were designed by belligerent drunk squirrels. Despite the sometimes massive amounts of technology and people involved in the process, I commonly see seasoned HRBPs and recruiters who have worked together for years act as if they've never seen this hiring process before. Who writes the job posting? Who should the hiring manager complain to when things take too long? Who is responsible for what?

Worse, these issues never seem to get solved, creating a process that has more in common with a patchwork of quick fixes and clear tape with little systemic thinking. When TA or HRIS installs a new element into the tech stack, it unravels the whole yarn ball, which ends up being hastily rewound in a new form because everyone is screaming that they need hires and hiring data yesterday.

This is why it often takes 2 years to change an ATS.

HRIS could be expected to manage this process, but their focus is on the tech itself: does it do what it is supposed to do? TA might manage the process, but few people became recruiters because of their deep love of enterprise tech. It's a gap that causes problems every day.

So I suggest you fix it.

This isn't a hard project, but it will feel like it at first. Here's what you do. Get TA leadership's approval to map the entire process. Talk to HR and get their approval to map the entire process. And then go make friends with the head of HRIS (this is your secret weapon later on because no one ever seems to remember HRIS and they have all the keys to the systems!) and get their permission to map the process.

It is highly likely that one or all these groups will say that there's already some type of process map. Don't believe them until you see it, walk the entire process, ask about 3 dozen stupid questions that start with, "and what happens here when…" or "why does this step happen here" or "is this step still true?" Chances are, the "map" is two generations old, and has been overrun with patches and fixes no one thought to document in the map.

Like a plumber in a brothel, we're not here to pass judgement, we're here to fix a problem.

When you map it, get in the weeds. Ask "why?" a lot. Ask "what happens if?" a lot. I mean, a lot a lot. Get annoying about it. And as you collect each step, you need to know a few things:

Who owns that step? This can be the person or the team responsible. If its a person, ask what happens when that person is on vacation. If its a team, ask how the tasks gets assigned to a person on that team.

How long does that step typically take? Some steps are simple. Click a button or send an email. But some can take weeks. You're not going to turn this into a Gantt chart and get your PMP project management certification. You're just trying to understand so you can explain it to someone else.

What screws this step up? Does this step need a signature? What happens when not enough people apply? What if the recruiter thinks the role is under-budgeted? What happens when the hiring manager adds or changes criteria to the job?

Systems are only as good as the people staffing it, and people are messy. Map the mess. Document every single step.

Once you're done, you should have a VERY long table in 4-5 columns mapping the process from the initial business need to the person stepping foot into the office and getting their badge (translate this to your own situation). You will likely note that the process is a very complicated dance between recruiting, hiring managers, HR, compensation and benefits, and HRIS. Each player has very different levels of power, interest and knowledge. For example, the hiring manager might have the most political juice, but in HR's world, they might be a beggar. The hiring manager might assume wanting the hire makes all the machinery go, and they just have to wait on the other end to catch the candidates as they come out. They don't want to understand the nuances of Comp&Ben (and really, who does?). They might not care that it can take a day or two for the newly minted job posting to hit all the major job boards. Like Veruca Salt (from Willy Wonka, not the rock band), they just want their candidate now.

At the same, HR and recruiting might not really understand (or feel) the cost of having a seat vacant. The hiring manager might be sweating bullets wondering how they will make their sales quota without a complete sales class that quarter, but the recruiter might not feel it.

Here's an example of what the final project might look like:

Step	Responsibility	Timeline	Notes
Hiring manager requests a requisition be opened by HR	Hiring Manager (HM)		

Step	Responsibility	Timeline	Notes
HR presumptively opens requisition	HRBP	As soon as possible, likely one day or less	
HRBP creates job description	HRBP	1-2 days, depending on if this is a new role or not	
Requisition is leveled and salary range applied	HRBP and Comp&Ben	Assume 3-4 days	HRBP will own this step, but will need C&B's input
Requisition is approved and sent to TA	HRBP	1 day	HRBP will alert HM that it is now in TA's hands
Recruiting leader assigns requisition to recruiter	TA Leadership	1 day	Based on function and workload
Recruiter sets up intake meeting with HM to understand who would make a good candidate	Recruiter	1-3 days	
Recruiter turns notes into job posting for ATS	Recruiter	1-2 days	
Job is posted into ATS	Recruiter	1 day	Job is automatically distributed to job boards
Recruiter sends job link to HM for review, and asks that the HM share link with team for referrals	Recruiter	1 day	

Step	Responsibility	Timeline	Notes
HM tells team and related departments about the opening and the bonus amount is for that referral	HM	0	Referrals are the #1 source of quality hires and speed the hiring process up
Recruiter reviews applications periodically for likely candidates for screening	Recruiter		
Continue through onboarding...			

Mapping this process has a number of positive impacts you will be taking advantage of shortly.

First, OMG there's a map!!! Once you finish the map, once you've got all the steps navigated and documented, present it back to TA, HR and HRIS. If you've done your job right, they will quibble. A lot. But you've asked all the hard questions and haven't mapped "what should be," but rather what truly is. When they tell you a step is wrong, pull out your notes and explain where your reasoning came from. Since you got your info from the people who actually do the work, you will have more credibility.

Second, OMG credibility out the wazoo! You are a master of the secret dark arts of hiring! Bow down! This is useful because often, employer branding can be seen as fluffy bunny stuff. But here you've built something real. It's like when the college professor stops lecturing for a second, reaches into the engine and correctly re-seats the distributor cap.

Third, this map will help you in your next project: turning the map into elevated recruiter presence. More on that in the next project.

Fourth, because you're no dummy, you might have noticed some places where the map shows problems. Or you think of ways to streamline the process because you're the only one who can see the complete picture. Slow play your fixes, but don't hide them. Trickle them out slowly, flexing your magical abilities to trim a step or a day from the hire. Remember, at some point, you will be wanting to show your impact in the form of shorter time to fill numbers. Why not stack the deck in your favor by fixing the mechanics of the process?

Finally, if you know the map, you can see all the different ways, places, processes and platforms you can tap into to insert your employer brand messages later. Knowing every step of the map means you can avoid spending money on new tools when you learn about an unused feature inside an existing program. Getting this close to the machine means you can start to slowly bend the machine to your will.

Anyway, this turns the mess into something understandable. Now you're going to turn it into something valuable.

BUILDING THE RECRUITER CHECKLIST

If you make friends with recruiters (or just buy them a drink), you'll hear the same complaints over and over. Sure, no one quite understands that they are the ones who find the talent that drives the business and thus should be more valued. Sure, being rejected by candidates a couple of dozen times a day can wear the skin off an elephant.

But the number one complaint is that their clients, the hiring managers, don't respect them.

You'll hear this expressed a number of different ways. They'll tell the story where no matter how many times they told the hiring manager that the talent wasn't out there for that salary, the hiring manager put their foot down and demanded the recruiter "just do it." They'll talk about how hiring managers try to set timelines for interviews, as if this is the only requisition the recruiter has. They'll talk about how diligently they prepare the candidate only to have the hiring manager staring at their phone through the interview as if the candidate didn't matter.

That can all be distilled into one phrase: Order-taker. That hiring managers see recruiters as nothing more than the person who brings the talent the hiring manager demands. Order-taker, someone with low skill or experience, a cog who's sole role is to select the obvious candidates from the pool of applicants and schedule the interview. Order-taker isn't so much as a slur as it is a shorthand that recruiters aren't valued or respected by their own clients.

It isn't because the recruiter is bad at their job. It's because what the hiring manager sees and what the recruiter is expected to do (and how they are expected to do it) are in misalignment. Recruiters are very much about methodically evaluating candidates quickly, building a temporary relationship with a stranger, getting a sense of who they are and how well they meet the stated and unstated expectations, and selling the role to the candidate, all in the space of minutes.

It is a kind of magic to be sure, but it is done on a retail level. Your job is to see things on a more systemic level. Which means you can offer help they can't offer themselves.

Remember, as the employer brand pro, you are on the side of the recruiter (for the moment), so let's see what we can do to help.

Have you ever called on a skilled tradesperson? Maybe an electrician or plumber to see about a problem you were having? Maybe it was an insurance adjuster or mechanic. If they show up with their hands in their pocket and ask, "what's the problem?" you might not feel very confident about their ability. They might be amazing at what they do, but they won't come across as prepared or experienced. They will come across as an order-taker.

Instead, if that person showed up with a clipboard and a series of checklists, asked you a series of predetermined questions to understand the problem from every angle, wouldn't you trust them more? Doesn't a doctor ask you a half dozen questions to understand your situation before asking, "what brought you in today?"

I'm not suggesting you buy lab coats for recruiters, but you can set them up for success by designing a new hire checklist.

Start with the above map. Strip out and/or bucket out the things that aren't about the recruiter or the hiring manager. For example, you don't need to show every step in the leveling or compensation processes. Start with the requisition's approval and what the recruiter does.

Here's an example checklist:

Step	TA	HM	Time
Schedule the Talent Strategy Meeting	X		Jan 3, 2020
Draft Talent Request Checklist	X		Jan 3, 2020
Talent Strategy Meeting, eview the job description for accuracy		X	Jan 5, 2020
Write public job posting	X		Jan 9, 2020
Approve job posting		X	Jan 10, 2020
Build job posting into ATS and push to the career site and job boards	X		Jan 10, 2020
Send link to HM with reminder about referrals	X		Jan 10, 2020
Send referral reminder to team		X	Jan 11, 2020
Post job posting to LinkedIn and other relevant social media channels		X	Jan 11, 2020
Review incoming applications and screen potential interview candidates	X		Jan 18, 2020
Determine if budget needs to be spent to promote this role	X		TBD
Present resumes to HM for consideratation	X		Feb 4, 2022
Give feedback on resumes		X	Feb 4, 2020
Schedule up interview loops	X		TBD
Schedule interview with HM (if HM cancels, HM will be responsible for rescheduling interview)	X		TBD
All parties in interview loops deliver completed feed-back on all candidates		X	TBD

Step	TA	HM	Time
Selection		X	TBD
Create and deliver offer	X		TBD
Negotiation		X	TBD
HR paperwork with start date		X	TBD

Additional information

Option	Selection
Do you prefer filling role faster or with best possible candidate	Faster
Who will be in the interview loop?	Name Name Name Optional name Alternate
If I have technical questions about the role, is there someone on your team who can answer my questions?	Name
Are we considering people outside the geographical area?	Yes
Can this role be 100% remote?	Potentially
Will you consider someone who applied in the past?	Yes

This checklist, once completed and used regularly, is the nerdiest magic you've ever seen. When the recruiter walks into the strategy meeting with a draft checklist, with initial times built in, they look like professionals who have their shit locked down. They look like the Seal Team of recruiting. Hiring managers will immediately treat the recruiter better.

Now, your job is to build a solid checklist based on your map. It needs to reflect reality and real processes.

And you'll need someone from TA leadership to look over your work to make sure it reflects their own expectations of how recruiters do their job.

The first time you present the checklist to a recruiter, they are probably going to look at you like you have three heads. So you'll need to sell them on this idea. Here's how:

Impact one: Immediate credibility and respect by the hiring manager. You can promise that using this checklist regularly will destroy any sense of being an order-taker the hiring manager feels about the recruiter.

Impact two: Setting roles and responsibilities. Did you see that some of these steps are owned by the hiring manager? Recruiters often complain that they have to wait for feedback on information from the hiring manager as if it doesn't impact the timeline or outcome. And let's be fair: recruiters are always measured on time to fill and hiring managers almost never are. This makes it clear that both parties are in it together and that they both impact the outcome.

Impact three: Less miscommunication. If a recruiter documents the intake meeting in their own chicken scratch, it is easy for a hiring manager to claim, "I never said that." Documenting it in a checklist that is reviewed together makes that impossible.

Impact four: Expectation setting. When the recruiter

and hiring manager go through this together, everyone understands how long steps take. The hiring manager knows that they will likely start seeing resumes in X weeks (instead of bugging the recruiter every day).

Impact five: Better change management in the future. Once everyone works to the checklist, adding or changing a step or tool is as easy as editing the checklist. Want to add a step where the hiring manager records a 30-second video from their laptop on why someone should apply? Add it to the checklist.

Like many projects with recruiters, you can't just dump it on their laps and expect them to clap. My strategy always starts by befriending one recruiter. Maybe two. When you hang out in weekly recruiting meetings (and yes, you really need to show up to those meetings), listen for who might be open to trying something new. Make friends with them and just start talking about their challenges. Get them to talk about hiring managers who just aren't useful, who like to throw expectations and demands around like they own the place. Say that you have an idea that you've heard has helped at other companies (which builds their interest), and would they help you try it out. That's when you show them the checklist.

At this stage, work closely with the recruiter to fine-tune the checklist. You want it bulletproof so that hiring managers don't feel like it's clunky. Ask the recruiter to try it out for at least the next three requisitions, just to see how it works. Then be supportive on the sidelines and see what happens.

What will likely happen is that the recruiter will notice a better relationship with the hiring manager, something closer to peers rather than servant. When they notice this, ask them to mention the experiment to other recruiters, perhaps at the next recruiting meeting.

Most recruiters won't listen to you, but they will absolutely listen to another recruiter. And when your new friend talks about how a simple change made an impact. Offer to share the checklist (and even tweak or customize it as needed) with more recruiters.

That's how you build momentum amongst recruiters: let them tout new ideas to recruiters for you. At least, in the beginning. Eventually, they will start to see you as a source of making recruiting better at the company and will listen to your ideas. But for now, let your cheerleaders promote the ideas.

Once the checklist really gets traction amongst the whole team, add one more element to the checklist: the signature.

At the bottom of all checklists, add a signature and date line for the hiring manager and recruiter. Once the checklist and dates have been completed, ask the hiring manager and recruiter to sign and date the checklist. While it isn't anywhere like a binding contract, it will feel like an agreement between peers, cementing expectations and responsibilities between parties.

ELEVATING RECRUITERS

Have you ever met someone and they had a commanding presence? They just lit up the room. They made you feel a little smaller but also a little warmer to be bathed in the light of their sun.

There are probably half a million products on the internet that will tell you that they know the secret of building rapport, to be the beating heart of any room, to command attention without saying a word. And those products will not have an easy way to give you a refund when they don't work.

To me, there isn't a silver bullet. There's no single magic "thing" you do to gain the respect of your peers and colleagues. It is a lot of little things that suggest that perhaps you are a woman with wit and panache or a man with style and grace then build on one another to reinforce that idea.

Hold on. I'm not suggesting that you learn these

tricks. I'm suggesting you teach them to recruiters.

More to the point, there are a number of small things you can suggest a recruiter do to help them elevate themselves or their hiring managers, to build respect and be treated as a peer, and not a minion or (gasp) order taker.

The first one is the easiest one. Suggest that the recruiter stop booking an "intake meeting" and instead call it a "Talent Strategy Meeting." Just calling the meeting an intake meeting suggests that the recruiter is only there to take in the hiring manager's order. Calling it a talent strategy meeting suggests that the recruiter is really a talent strategist, someone who understands the ins and outs of the talent market, knowing how hard it is to find certain skill sets and what they generally pay.

The next one goes along with the previous one. When the recruiter books the talent strategy meeting, have the calendaring program automatically add a draft agenda to the meeting. Maybe it just says:

1. Review the status of current open roles
2. Review the job description for accuracy and necessity
3. Set expectations for talent volume
4. Review the checklist and establish anticipated timeline for this role

Setting the agenda means you have the power and

authority to set the agenda. Having power means you are more likely to be seen as a peer to the hiring manager. Just dropping in this agenda elevates the recruiter.

Oh, and if you can figure out how to make that agenda just pop in, either with a sticky key or a shortcut or a template within the calendar and install it on the recruiter's computer without them even lifting a finger, you'll get so many extra points.

Next, the recruiter brings along a printed copy of the recruiter checklist. The first time a recruiter goes through this process with a hiring manager, the checklist should be blank, only containing the steps of the process.The recruiter will walk the hiring manager through the process and explain any steps that are unclear, putting check marks in the column to designate whether it is the responsibility of the recruiter or the hiring manager and the adding draft or temporary dates on the the first few lines. Once the meeting is over, the recruiter can complete a digital version of the checklist and email it to the hiring manager, thus cementing the relationship and responsibilities on both sides.

By doing this, it tells the hiring manager that this is a truly collaborative process and if they don't do their part, they won't get the right candidate in a timely manner. The next time the recruiter comes to an "talent strategy meeting" (nee "intake meeting"), the recruiter should have the responsibility columns filled out and maybe even some initial dates to review.

Once all recruiters have this process down, encourage the recruiting leader to go back and see how closely actual hire dates correlated with anticipated hire dates. Some recruiters might be overly optimistic in their planning and a minor tweak will help them look more credible over time.

JOB POSTINGS THAT ACTUALLY DON'T SUCK

Have you seen the recent reboot of Sherlock? The one with Benedict Cumberbatch and Martin Freeman? The best part is, of course, when Sherlock takes a glance at someone and immediately ascertains and infers all sorts of amazing information about them - that they just got married, that thet recently quit smoking, that they recently traveled abroad, etc.

I kind of feel the same way about job postings. When I read them, I feel like I can see so much information that was never meant to be in the posting, and most of it unflattering. For example, I can see when the job posting was stolen from some other place, like a book or job description. Or from another company (yes, I've seen it). I can tell when the hiring manager doesn't talk to the recruiter. I can tell how arrogant the hiring manager is by how little information is in the posting. I can tell when someone from creative was enlisted to help write it. I can tell how much of a stranglehold the internal comms team has over the processes.

That is to say, job postings, which are often done almost without any real intention, reveal so much of the company. As you are the owner of how people perceive the brand, you need to take ownership of this process. And because job postings are most used internally by recruiters, you need to make sure you own them in a way that supports the recruiters.

First, this caveat.

JOB DESCRIPTIONS ARE LEGAL DOCUMENTS. JOB POSTINGS ARE MARKETING MATERIALS.

Ahem.

Job descriptions are legal documents owned by legal and HR and I do not in any way suggest making any changes whatsoever to them. They are there to help the company avoid lawsuits and do… well, whatever HR does all day.

You know you're reading a job posting because it sounds like two lawyers who don't like each other trying to describe something they've never seen, with the resulting text translated into Icelandic and back again. No one should ever want to read one of these unless paid well. Certainly not a job candidate.

Job postings, by contrast, are marketing documents. When done poorly, they may make use of some of the language from the job posting (mistake!), but they aren't bound by the same legal guidelines as a legal document. That is, you should think of the job posting as a way to get the right person excited to do the job and let the description serve as technical documentation.

Setting that aside for just a moment, job postings are almost always the first interaction someone has with your employer brand, which is why failing to write better job postings isn't just a missed opportunity, it makes your job harder down the road. You'll be forced to spend time and energy and political capital trying to build things to neutralize the bad impression the job posting left on candidates.

Because they are the first impression, a better job posting allows you to set the frame around the company. It is how you plant your flag to your brand position, the thing your career site, social media posts, Glassdoor responses, interview questions and marketing collateral should validate. Without this frame, you are just making various potentially-related claims about the company and asking candidates to interpret what they see. That's a mistake you don't need to make.

And the best part of writing your own job postings is that they are free!!! There are few other ways you have to make a huge impression on candidates that only cost you some time and thought to write things up.

Not writing better job postings is a travesty. It is as if you are telling the world, "I don't care that I smell horrible. I don't care that showers are all but free. I don't care that the stench offends you. I just don't care." Frankly, after reading a lot of job postings, it's almost a wonder any applies to a job at all

Finally, for most recruiters, writing job postings is one of the worst parts of their job. Taking responsibility (mostly) out their hands is better than bringing donuts to work.

The problem is that when we write a job posting, we are only trying to write one job posting, one for that specific role. But tomorrow, a new requisition will appear. And the day after and the week after that.

When you're at home and you decide to bake a loaf of bread, it becomes a time-consuming and messy process to produce one loaf of bread. But a professional baker doesn't make one loaf of bread, they build systems to build lots of bread effectively and efficiently.

Be the baker.

So here's my eight-point model for building job postings at something closer to scale, so that each subsequent new posting takes less time than the previous one.

1.   Headline
2.   1st Paragraph: Describe the change the company is seeking to make in the world

3. 2nd Paragraph: Describe how the team is supporting the company to make that change
4. 3rd Paragraph: Describe how the role is supporting the team
5. 4th Paragraph: Describe the micro-culture of the team or office
6. Bullet Section: How you'll spend your time here...
7. Bullet Section: We'd love to talk to you if you have many of the following...
8. Use the "Magic bullets" for the last two sections

Let's break that down.

Headline

The headline is how you grab a job seeker's attention and set the frame for the rest of the engagement. If your brand is all about prestige, ask if someone feels like they are getting the attention at their current job they deserve. If your brand is all about respect, ask if the candidate feels truly respected at work and can bring their whole self there. For the rest of the engagement (job posting, career site, screener questions, interview questions, offer letter, etc) you will be paying out against the idea planted here. So nail it.

I would suggest that asking a question in the headline commands its own attention. If you see a question out in the wild, your brain automatically tries to answer the question, even if you don't realize it. This means that a question generally gets more mental cycles spent on it than something that's purely "look at me!"

Also, the goal of the headline is not to define the job, but to entice the candidate to read more. That's all. If you explain what the job is in the headline, why would they want to read more?

Finally, you might notice that your ATS doesn't have a field called "Headline." That's fine. Almost ever ATS allows for simple HTML, so wrap your headline in this code: <h1></h1> so that it looks like this:

<h1>This is a headline</h1> This is the beginning of the first paragraph...

The <h1> will make whatever text between the tags big and bold. And if the job gets pushed to a job board that doesn't support <h1> tags, it will just look like the very first line of the posting.

1st Paragraph: Company

Don't get this wrong. You might be inclined to just steal some text from the "About Us" page on the corporate site and trim to fit. That is a bad idea.

The goal here (and as we go through the model, you'll understand why) is to establish the change the company is attempting to make in the universe. It doesn't matter if it's to bring more flavors of the mediterranian to tables around the world, or make it easier for people around the world to buy dog food. What is the purpose of the company framed as a change they are trying to make.

If you let the comms team write this, you aren't going to get the impact you need. They will fill it with details that doesn't entice anyone to apply. Does it matter that the company was founded in 2009? Does it matter that the company went public in 2017? Are you going to apply because it has two thousand employees instead of three thousand? Of course not. But that's the kind of thing you'll get stuck with if you let someone else make the first draft. So write the first draft by yourself and ask the comms team what changes they need to make it align with their needs as well as be factually accurate.

The nice thing about this model is that this paragraph can (and should) be re-used as the first paragraph for every job posting hereafter. Nailing this section automatically makes the next posting easier to write because it's already partly written.

But remember, while you don't have to be a creative genius copywriter, you want to make this company description interesting enough that the reader wants to read the next paragraph.

2nd Paragraph: Team
The second paragraph should describe how this particular team supports the team in its goal of changing the world. It doesn't matter what team it is, from coding or sales to admin or custodial services, how does this team help the company change the world?

This paragraph allows us to connect the dots between any given role and the goal and purpose of the company, thus clarifying why this role is important.

Once you write any team paragraph, you can re-use that team paragraph for every role within that team. See how you're shrinking the amount of time and effort any one job posting requires?

3rd Paragraph: Role

By now you've guessed that this paragraph describes how the role plays an important role in supporting the team. Feel free to throw in information around what other teams this role works with, how its impact is measured and specific traits that someone might need to be successful.

The magic of this model is that it makes it clear to the reader how this role plays a role in the company, regardless of the role.

4th Paragraph: Culture or Location

If the first three paragraphs are what the role does, this is the paragraph that describes how the work gets done. Is this role designed to be collaborative or solo? Does this team tend to be very friendly with each other, or is it more professional? Do they compete with each other? Is that competition friendly or more cut-throat? Does this team work long hours, or is the goal to be home by six? Don't feel like you need a complete psychological workup on the team, but identify some key traits common with the team to help the candidate better understand what they might be getting into.

Again, having written this once, reuse it for every relevant team and location.

How you'll spend your time here

Most job postings call this section "Responsibilities," suggesting that grumpy lawyers and disappointed parents wrote this job posting, impacting people's sense of the brand (and you're in charge of that, remember?). I much prefer to change this to some variation on "What a typical day looks like."

By changing the label, not only do you make the tone more friendly, you alleviate the necessity to be somehow 100% comprehensive, which is impossible (which is why so many job postings end with "and other duties as assigned" which is the biggest cop-out in all of HR). Instead, think about how you're painting a picture of what working here might be like. Leave enough room in the description for the candidate to project themselves into the role, trying it on like a new sweater to see how it fits.

Make sure to write as many of the bullets as possible in the "magic bullets" format, which I'll describe in a moment.

We'd love to talk to you if you have many of the following

Normally, this section is called "Qualifications" or "Requirements" and that is problematic. Aside from having all the warmth of your average bench warrant, these terms can encourage more men than women to apply. How? Statistics show that if there are six "requirements" in a job posting, a man who only meets five of them, will still apply where a woman is more likely to assume she isn't qualified and not apply. Changing the language can encourage more women and other diverse audiences to apply.

I will admit I don't have the data to back this up, but I do have anecdotal evidence. Sephora, the makeup retailer, has a development team that is 70% women. This is an industry where having 10% women is unusual. If you go look at their job postings, you'll see that they use this kind of language.

Magic Bullets

I know that calling them "magic bullets" makes me sound crazy, but I swear by these. Let me show you what I mean.

In a typical job posting, you might see a "requirement" that's worded as, "Must have intermediate experience in Excel." Somehow, we're all expected to understand what that means, but it isn't even remotely clear. There is no standard for "intermediate" Excel skills. If I don't know much about Excel, I might think that knowing how to write a basic formula is pretty intermediate, while someone with a lot more experience might consider VLOOKUP or pivot tables to be an intermediate skill.

Also, when a job posting lists a bunch of bullets, it gets to be a bit… onerous. It feels like the hiring manager is building a wishlist of skills without considering who might have them all. Generally, standard bulleted lists push people away rather than describe or attract.

But there is a better way. Follow this formula:

You will [SKILL] to [TASK] in order to [OUTCOME or PURPOSE]

Watch how this formula works against our Excel example.

"Must have intermediate experience in Excel" becomes "You will use Excel to build pivot tables in order to identify sales opportunities."

Okay, aside from sounds far more human and engaging, the magic bullet formula does a few more things. First, it clarifies what you mean by "intermediate Excel." There's no misunderstandings here. Second, it keeps the bullet from sounding like a wishlist item, because the candidate can see exactly how that skill will be used in the job. Finally, this model reinforces all the points you've been making about how this makes an impact on a larger stage because the candidate can see exactly what they will have to do to make that impact.

Here's another example. My guess is that 80-90% of

all job postings have a variant of the following: "must have excellent written and verbal skills." This suggests that the role may be required to occasionally write dialog for a screenplay and deliver flawless tongue-twisters. Maybe the role will need to deliver keynote speeches or write profound haiku. It's unclear.

Instead, you could write the same bullet as, "You will write emails and communicate with remote employees in order to ensure that expectations and guidelines are delivered." Suddenly, I understand what the role looks like more clearly and I don't have to worry about whether my lack of iambic pentameter experience will be a hindrance to my success.

You don't have to make every bullet into this format, but focus on the first few. Or at least the two or three most important skills or tasks.

So why are we deciding to become responsible for the job postings? So glad you asked!

One, if this is the first impression of the brand most people get, are you going to let someone else write that first impression for you? Someone who is so busy they are more likely to steal text from a different job (or company) before thinking about your own brand? If you answered, "yes," get out now. I can't help you.

Two, taking this off recruiters' plates will make you a lot of friends in the TA team. Beyond giving them a little time back, ask if they notice a difference in the quality of candidates who apply. Remember, recruiters won't listen to you, but they will listen to other recruiters. Getting them to tell each other that these work encourages adoption.

Three, while this seems time consuming, it really is an investment. Build a proper system and install it and maintain it and it will yield value to you forever. It will attract the right kinds of applicants and repel the others. It will plant the brand seed that you'll be paying off throughout the rest of the candidate experience and beyond. And as you influence who applies, you are really influencing who gets hired (hiring managers mostly choose amongst those who apply, and those who apply saw something in the job posting they liked), so this is how you change the company culture over the (very) long term.

So once you prove that rearranging letters on a screen can help attract better candidates faster and easier, you should start thinking about how to expand that idea to recruiting outreach.

OUTREACH MESSAGES

Author secret: I wrote this section last because I knew it would probably be the hardest to write. Having once been in the position of being able to just toss off cute outreach messages that were different for the sake of being different, I now am somewhat tempered, having spent more than a year writing cold emails to potential prospects on the sales side.

Outreach messages are hoodoo. They are expected to attract just enough attention to make someone read more, which means being specific enough to make the person reading it not think its a generic pitch mass mailed to the world. They walk an almost flirtatious, almost invisible line between promise and come on, planting the idea of a wonderful future they aren't in a position to deliver, all amongst the backdrop of dozens of other recruiters making similar pitches. They are professional witchcraft, talismans to scare the demons and draw in the righteous souls to a good company.

These are impossible positions to put recruiters in.

But the outreach message is the primary way for a lot of companies to source talent. In a few sentences, they need to make a complete stranger open up their minds to a new way of seeing the world, a world in which they have a different job.

Now, in the face of such an impossible task, some recruiters play ostrich, write a "good enough" outreach message, bake it into their spam tool of choice and get to work, like a blindfolded hunter, shooting at every noise that sounds like prey.

Many recruiters will face such crushing rejection with something I would label "shame." Their outreach doesn't work, they don't know why it doesn't work, and they won't show other recruiters what they are doing for fear of… I don't really know. Being laughed at? Realizing that no one's really got it figured out? I don't know. But these recruiters will protect and guard their messaging, making it almost impossible to improve.

And in this mix, making everything even more complicated, are the hucksters and hounds, pitching workshops and books to help recruiters write "outreach messages that work." They make promises that never materialize, and personally, I think they feed the fear, confusion and shame recruiters grapple with because only rarely does anyone acknowledge that they are in an impossible position.

So here is my recommendation to you. If you want to help steer recruiters away from spammy and pitchy outreach, you need to find a way to do it collectively. You need to focus on facilitating a semi-regular meeting where you work with all recruiters to brainstorm outreach messages.

You can't walk in the meeting thinking you're clever enough to have all the answers (as this author has been guilty of), but to help provide a different perspective.

Here are the lessons I propose you share and work through with them:

One: The subject line is not the pitch. It is an invitation to the content. As we talk in other sections, the goal is simply to get a stranger to stop and consider and give them a reason to continue. Nothing more. For a job where they were now looking out of town for a high-level candidate, Once I confirmed that they anticipated flying the candidate in for an interview, I pitched a subject line that just said, "Would you be interested in a free trip to Chicago?' The rest of the message would clarify that come on, but it would be interesting enough to grab attention and stand out.

Two: Get past the obvious. Once you get everyone one into the room, everyone must throw out an idea, even if it is a dumb idea. Your goal is to build the muscle where recruiters learn to get past the obvious outreach message. What's wrong with the obvious message? Because that's what prospects are likely seeing from every other recruiter in the world. Unless you're already widely known as a great company to work for, you need to stand out a little. That starts with a better outreach message.

Three: It's about them, not you. The biggest mistake in any outreach message (as the target of thousands of them), is that they are all about the recruiter and the company sending it rather than about the prospect. Why should I be impressed that you're a great place to work, when you don't show how it's a great place to work for me? While every outreach blog post and survey says that personalized messages perform better, it takes more than head-nodding to some comment made on LinkedIn or Github. It means that you've spent a few minutes trying to understand this person and what they might want. IT's not easy, but it works better.

Four: We is better than me. There is power in the group. A bad idea gets a chuckle, but someone else turns it around and suddenly it is a brand new way to think about what the candidate might want or how to present it. Having a meeting where everyone is safe to try something new, (and following it up to see how the ideas went) is how you instill a willingness to change.

Five: Don't forget the brand. This isn't about inserting talking points to turn every recruiter into a mynah bird, but instead, put together a lexicon of 20-30 words that feel like the brand, that suggest a way of seeing the world that helps connect the message to the job posting to the career site to the LinkedIn post to the Glassdoor response to the interview request to the interview question and to the offer letter. Those words make it easy for each recruiter to support the brand (see? I didn't forget about your day job) without having to run everything by you.

But like I mentioned, writing outreach is a muscle you need to help strengthen. And like your own body, you don't get fit going to the gym once, but by making it a regular habit. So keep booking the meetings (or include it once a month during the regular recruiters meeting).

MAKE ANY REFERRAL PROGRAM BETTER

When people start getting into photography, they tend to get a little fixated on the equipment. What kind of camera body should they get? What kind of lens? How many lenses? Tripod or not? It is very easy to get wrapped up in one body versus another as to which would take the best picture.

But professional photographers have a saying: the best camera is the one to have in your hand.

The saying is there to remind you to not get lost in the features but focus on the purpose of what the camera is there to do: capture a moment in time.

I need to start by saying that I am 100% agnostic when it comes to what kind of referral program you should use. In the same way the best camera is the one in your hand, the best referral program or system is the one you've got.

And that's the problem I have with almost every referral program. They seem to equate features with usefulness. Does it matter if the referral program is mobile friendly if no one wants to download the app? Does it matter if a referral can be made in two clicks if no one remembers where the buttons are?

I take a different approach. I think referral program effectiveness isn't based on the tool but on how it is communicated to staff.

Most referral projects follow a similar path: Spend a few months picking the "best" program, working with HRIS to install and integrate the program, training recruiters how to see or find the referral, and then launching the program to the company. That launch will be a company-wide email with a lot more instructions on how to use the tool than reasons why anyone should want to refer a friend. The documentation will be stored on the intranet in a place that even god would need a bloodhound to track down.

For ten seconds after they see the email asking if they know of "anyone great" the employee will rack their brain for... well, gosh it isn't clear. Does the company need great developers? Sales people? Writers? Managers? What roles is the company trying to fill? Oh, then they have to go to some other web site to figure that out? And then they have to come back and connect the role to my friend? Suddenly, everyone's lost interest.

Ten minutes after the launch, no one will remember having seen the email and the program will collect dust. Oops.

Instead of a big launch (which no one will remember), go micro instead of macro. Rather than a big launch, focus on telling people about the program at the moment when they need to know. Don't rely on their memory, build a system. And make it specific.

The reason why referral programs fail is that they aren't very specific. HR might know exactly how to refer someone, how much the referral bonus is for a given hire, how and when it gets paid out, and who's eligible, but most staff don't. So unless all your referrals come from HR, you've got an issue.

Instead, ask yourself when someone might need to know about the referral program. Probably when the role opens, right? And rather than have HR send out a reminder (not to be the jerk here, but have you ever gotten a mass email from HR and thought to yourself, "I bet this is useful information I need right away!"? Probably not), have someone's boss send it out. And not just anyone, send that reminder to people who will likely know great candidates.

Yeah, that probably sounded like gobbledygook. Let me show you what you should install and it should become pretty clear.

When the job goes live on the ATS and is being pushed out to job boards (a job posting you helped write, I hope), the recruiter probably writes an email to the hiring manager to say things are in progress. This is the moment where all the elements are ripe for a referral.

Ask the recruiter to add in language asking the hiring manager to remind their team about the referral program. Link to the actual role. List the specific bonus. Maybe even throw in a line about who would be a great candidate. The hiring manager copies that language and pastes it into an email to all their reports, people who are best positioned to know who would make a great fit for the team.

Remember: people are fairly tribal. If you want to hire an electrician, don't talk to a recruiter. Talk to another electrician. The same is true for salespeople, product managers, coders, admins, and even recruiters. This process allows you to tap into the right network at the right time with all the relevant information necessary for them to take action. That's the secret of a strong referral program.

Here's an example email you can send to the hiring manager:

[name],

Your job posting for [ROLE] is now live at [URL to the opening on your ATS].

Please copy the following text to your entire team. You can edit it, but it should help increase referrals, which will help us close this requisition faster.

Thanks!

Team,

As you probably know, we're looking to hire a new [ROLE] into our team. If you know of someone who would be a good fit, be sure to submit a referral of their name and email address here [LINK TO REFERRAL TOOL]. If your connection gets hired, you'll be getting a referral bonus of [AMOUNT OF BONUS] in [TIMELINE].

Thanks!

Obviously, you should feel free to re-write this email for your recruiters. But just making this tweak will do more to promote long-term referral rates than pretty much any other variable (including referral tool).

There's an ancillary impact here, as well. This kind of templated email system makes it crystal clear what the hiring manager should do to increase their own chances of finding a great hire faster. As we'll see in the social media section, you can add on to this email to encourage those hiring managers to push the open role out to their own networks easily.

Now, if you ask all the recruiters to comply with this

new process, don't be surprised for some pushback, especially if you haven't built trust and relationships with the recruiters. Instead, suggest that this is an extension of the checklist process that turns recruiters from order-takers into talent strategists in the eyes of hiring managers.

Using your email template, bake the text into each recruiter's computer (either as a template within the email program or as automated text). Show how following this process reinforces the perception of professionalism, but also increases the number of qualified referrals that will come in.

Caveat: I don't have any sense how wide-spread this attitude is, but some recruiters actually hate referrals. They have gotten too many junk referrals (unqualified cousins from leadership or people who submit everyone they've ever met in the hopes of landing referral bonuses) and now see referrals as useless. In this case, you might need to talk to HRIS and pull referral data to tell a different story about referral candidates.

What is interesting here is that leadership is investing in referrals, but the boots on the ground are ignoring the strategy. You might need to loop in the head of TA or even the CHRO to sort things out.

But you might be wondering how better referrals help you achieve your employer brand goals. That's a valid question.

But allow me to answer a question with a question: What do all successful companies have in common? A high referral rate. Why? If people love working somewhere, they want to bring in more of their favorite people. Thus, a high referral rate is a huge indication that you have a strong employer brand. So if you are going to add "internal referral rate" as one of your KPIs (and I'd suggest doing that), don't leave it to chance: build a better referral process. This is a great way to show your impact without spending any money and making your recruiting team look like rockstars (while decreasing their workload through some simple automation).

ALUMNI PROGRAM

It used to be that when someone left the company, they were effectively dead. They were forgotten. Like former dictators, their images and name were stricken from websites and social media. This idea made a kind of twisted sense in the days when you were expected to work in the same company for most of your life. But that hasn't been true in… decades? Generations? So let's let this strange idea die.

I mean, here are people who spent time in the company, who have an insider's view of how things work, who would be happy working in the company, and a network of people in similar roles who would be willing to hear all about their experiences.

Call me crazy, but getting these people to not talk smack about the company because of a decades out-of-date custom sounds like an employer brand problem to me, doesn't it? So let's fix it.

Now, you probably won't be able to change the thinking of all your old school and hard-core team leads who take every person leaving as some kind of personal betrayal (and yes, there are still plenty of people like that), you can take advantage of the system you mapped (or, as you should be referring to it, "the gift that just keeps on giving") and plant a positive brand message in people walking out the door.

Heck, you might even encourage them to send referrals back to the company. Or even boomerang! But we'll get to that in a bit.

The first step is to talk to those unsung heroes in HRIS and ask how the HR management system is notified that someone is giving notice and what their end date will be. This is crucial for a few reasons. First, you want to automate everything you can. Once automated, you can focus on the next project knowing that this is going to keep helping you plant those messages. Second, this allows you to filter out people who were fired. I'm not saying that people who are laid off or fired for cause aren't allowed to have a voice, but that HR will likely try to quash your project unless you can show that you aren't including those folks.

Once HRIS can isolate the step in the HR management system, you should build an automated email to those people who are leaving. I don't have a good sense of timing, if this should hit their inboxes the day after they announce or the day before they leave for good. Just pick a reliable date. Let HRIS offer advice and listen to them.

Here's an example email you should bake into the system:

> Dear [FIRST NAME],
>
> Someone once said something about how parting was a sweet sorrow, and it still rings true. On one hand, we're all thrilled to see you move to the next step in your professional journey, but we're also sad to see you go.
>
> But this doesn't have to be the end of the relationship. Since you have so much experience at [COMPANY], you have a valuable perspective on who would be successful and fulfilled working here. If you ever run into anyone who would be a great match, please send them our way.
>
> And if you don't mind, we'd like to stay connected with you. It doesn't have to be a big deal, but if you join out [COMPANY] Alumni Group, you can stay a part of the company alumni community and the professional networks therein. Who knows, maybe one day you'd like to come back! That would be amazing. Here's the link [URL].
>
> Anyway, we wish you all the success in the world and hope that you found your time here as a formative and useful experience.
>
> Best of luck,
>
> Your friends and colleagues at [COMPANY]

It doesn't take much to create an emotional connection to make sure that the soon-to-be-former staff sees their time there positively. Just this kind of email will help elevate exit interview and ratings website scores. And since your Glassdoor (or your rating site of choice) score is probably part of your KPIs, this will help.

Now, you might have noticed that the email lists an alumni group, the thought of which might give you terror sweats. Not to worry. If you keep your expectations low, you can build and manage an alumni group (not a "community," suggesting a place where you expect to spark and manage a lot of two-way conversation which sounds, frankly, exhausting) with low work and the potential for high yield.

The first question to answer is: Facebook or LinkedIn? Now, for my money (and as of this writing), they aren't that different. LinkedIn Groups (on-and-off-again supported by LinkedIn) have a professional credibility built in. Pretty much most people are "on" LinkedIn, so asking them to follow the group isn't asking much. But Facebook has far better community tools, allowing you to engage in conversation and monitor threads and posts in real time. For me, for groups in which I expect to have a lot of engagement, Facebook Groups are hands-down better groups. But that might not be the right answer for you. Picking Facebook doesn't mean anyone will post, but because most people don't see Facebook as a professional resource, it might be tough to use it as a way for people to show pride in their former employer.

Either way, lock the group down so that strangers aren't allowed to join and post. This is your watering hole and you don't want other companies to poach from it! Put a weekly meeting on your calendar where you review the people who have requested to join. Just confirm that they used to work at your company (this is easier on LinkedIn where they will have their professional history in their profile), and approve admittance. Once or twice a month, post something into the group about the company.

You might even start things off by searching LinkedIn for people who used to work there. Ask them to join in a super simple message like:

> Hi!
>
> As a former employee of [COMPANY], you might want to join the alumni group. It would be a great way to network with other people who found success beyond [COMPANY].
>
> Thanks!

That's it. Super simple.

You might be wondering what this has to do with recruiters. Great question! Once you've got the group going, once the automation is recommending the group to people leaving, let recruiting leadership know that you are fostering this group. When recruiters are running into roadblocks or need to source candidates, it is a whole bunch of people who already know the brand and the kinds of people you hire.

You can either post new openings to the group (be judicious in what you post - you don't want it to feel like a janky craigslist), or you can reach out to group members and ask if they can recommend and refer someone.

By building and maintaining the resource of connections (and even potential hires), recruiting will see you as a strategist there to help them get work done better and faster.

That's a good place to be.

BUILDING REGULAR CONTENT

There is no tagline, commercial, jingle or ad that connects with people better than a good story. Stories are remembered better and longer. They can be internalized and repurposed any number of ways to attract a specific audience. They can be sliced, diced and reformed any number of ways to suit.

Stories are freaking magical.

They are, however, somewhat hard to build.

Wait. That's not actually true. Stories exist everywhere, you just have to look. Stories are being told by everyone, you just have to ask. Stories can take any shape or size, you just have to polish them up a little.

So in this section, I will show you how to build a legitimate story-creating and content-generating machine. It will cost you slightly more than nothing. You just have to build it, work it, and maintain it and the content will flow pretty much forever.

When you want to build a story of some soft today, let's say a medium-sized blog post, how long does it take to build? Maybe you have to figure out what story you want to tell. Or maybe you just have to find someone to interview. Then you interview them and take copious notes. Then you review your notes and try to turn hash into steak. Then you show the story to the interviewee to make sure you captured it correctly, Then you lay the story out into a blog post. Then you have to find an image. Then you push it out.

How long does that take? 8 hours? 10? More?

If you follow the directions here, you'll build a machine that builds a great profile with about as many words as a blog post in about 45 minutes. There's some investment of time and technology at the front end, but once it's in place, content almost seems to create itself. In fact, you'll go from having to beg people to help you create a story, to becoming selective as to what content you push and when.

True story. Here's how you can do it, too.

Step One: Make a Form
I'm cheap, so I used a Google form, but it literally doesn't matter what you use. At first, the form will be dead simple, but once you get some experience with it, by the time you hit Step Nine, you'll be able to do some cool tricks with it.

In the form, start by writing a paragraph explaining what this form is and how you plan to use their responses. You'll end up rewriting this paragraph often the first few months as more people become familiar with it, but to start, you want to create as much clarity and certainty as you can. An example paragraph might look like this:

> Hi!
>
> Thanks so much for helping out the employer brand team by telling us a little more about yourself. First, a few notes.
>
> One, we aren't here to make you look bad. We want to showcase you and your work in your own voice. We'll edit things, so feel free to share complete stories as you can.
>
> Two, most fields are optional, so if you don't want to answer one or two, no big deal. Three, you were chosen because someone thinks you have an interesting story to share. So don't second-guess things. Just share.
>
> If you have any questions, just ask [NAME].
>
> Thanks!

Use your own language and tone. This paragraph sets the frame for the rest of the form, and at the beginning, your problem will likely be pulling enough info out of someone rather than editing. As people start to see what their answers are turning into, this won't be as necessary.

Next, collect some basic logistical stuff: name, department, office location, start month, what ERGs they are connected to, if they've won any awards, etc.

But the real meat is in the questions and prompts you use. Bad questions won't encourage people to share, so you need to design questions that don't just elicit funny or clever answers, but align to your overall concept of the brand (which is why you're building this in the first place: to build the proof points that validate your brand). Here are some of my favorite questions, but they won't all be appropriate for every brand. So steal as much as you want, but think about how you'd tailor or re-think your questions to suit.

- What does your mom think you do all day?
- What's the best piece of advice you've ever gotten from a boss here?
- Tell the story of something challenging you faced here and how you solved the problem.
- Who or what inspires you?
- How do you see your work impacting the company mission?
- What's the proudest moment you've had here?
- What's something interesting about you most people don't know?
- If you could do another job here for one day, what would it be and why?
- Write a haiku about working here
- What advice would you have for someone just starting out here?
- What surprised you most when you started here?
- If your teammates gave you an award, what superlative award would you get?

- In three words, describe your team
- If you are a boomerang, what brought you back?

Now, you will tweak these questions a lot over the first few months. And when we get to Step Nine, you'll likely end up asking different questions of people in different teams. But for now, this might be just enough to get the ball rolling.

Pro tip: At the end of the form, add a checkbox that says, "by checking this box, I grant [COMPANY] the right to use my likeness/voice/name/comments for external use. Checking this box will act as your signature." This keeps everything nice and legal. (I AM NOT A LAWYER!!! Talk to your own legal department to do it right for you.)

Step Two: Share the Form

As an employer brand, you probably have a few internal cheerleaders you go to for help. They get what you're doing and love to help out. These are your guinea pigs.

Try to put together a list of about ten cheerleaders and send this email to them (send it individually, not en masse):

Hi!

You know what? You're great. You've been an amazing help to me and the employer brand team and I would love to ask one more favor of you. Well, it's really not a favor. I'd really like to make you a little more famous in the company.

Intrigued? I hope so.

I'd like you to fill out a survey for me, It shouldn't take more than 15 minutes, but it isn't a standard form. It will ask you about your experiences working here. Please fill out as much of the form as you feel comfortable doing and I promise to make you look great.

Sound good? Here's the link: [URL]

Thanks so much for being such a supporter of the brand and I look forward to your answers to the form!

Now, here's the honest truth. If you send this to ten people, 3-5 will ignore you. If 5-7 people will it out, you'll only get 2-3 usable submissions. That's just how it is at first. As people see what you're building, you'll be surprised at how that conversion rate shifts in your favor. Just know that you need to ask ten people to get enough people to get things moving.

So pick the best response and move to step three.

Step Three: Build the Platform
If you're cheap like me, you need to get familiar with Wordpress, the content management system that powers the bulk of the internet (no fooling!). But it's a pretty easy tool once you get used to it, and it has all

sorts of ways to extend the functionality.

The reason I suggest Wordpress is that it's free (yay!), it has tagging functionality (so you can tag each person with their team and office location and then it will show all people from that office or team, stuff that will be amazingly useful once you get a few dozen profiles made), and you can build templates.

Templates are wonderful, because you're going to spend this time perfecting the look and feel of the template so that every new form submission can be copy and pasted into the template in about five minutes, making the "content creation" process insanely fast.

I don't want to get into the gory details of Wordpress (and if your company has a CMS its using, I guess you're better off using something with some internal support), but here's what you need to make:

- One home page
- One about page
- One profile template (but start it off as a page)

That's it. Get these three things right and everything will come from these. For example, if your D&I gets wind of this and wants to build an D&I page, clone the About Us page and ask them for images and content. Boom. Done.

Later on, once things are settled, start playing around

and seeing what cool things you can add in. This is a living, breathing site, so treat it as such. It will never be "done," so be willing to push it out while it's a little rough knowing you can polish and tweak later.

Step Four: Template a single profile

Your profile template should start with the content from a completed form (remember when I told you to pick your favorite response? Yay, use that) so that you've got a real world example. Build the page with all the questions baked in. Give the questions a slightly different look and feel so it's obvious to a reader that this is a Q&A model.

In fact, picking fonts and kerning and text treatments will take a little time. Show what you're working to someone in a design/creative team and ask for feedback. If they make suggestions you don't understand, ask if it would be easier for them to login and tweak to make it work. Design and creative folks love to get their hands dirty, so let them.

Next, figure out how you want to display the logistics/metadata. For me, I put the name, team and office as the headline. Then I put the rest of the metadata (start month, awards) in a little sidebar. But design it how you like.

Finally, figure out where the images go.

Come back!!!

First off, images don't have to be hard. I took headshots of people in the C-suite with an iPhone 6 that looked amazing. The secret is getting good lighting. My suggestion is to find a place in the office that gets a lot of light and try to face your subject towards the light without blinding them. Set your camera such that the background gets a little blurry (which makes a\ny picture look like a pro took it), and then take a dozen pictures. In fact, never stop hitting the big button. Even if you suck, with good lighting and enough chances, something good will come out.

I used the glossy headshot as the banner image (and the "featured image" if you're using Wordpress), but then I would ask for goofy pics from their own social media and phone. I'd sprinkle those throughout the profile to give more personality and leverage pictures they already thought made them look good. The goal is to keep this simple for everyone.

Then start showing the page off internally. Ask for feedback. Take a look at how it looks on a phone and a mac and a PC. Ask people what would make it better. You're not beholden to listen to anyone, but this is the best way to crowd-source out any mistakes before you really launch things. As someone who hates to hear feedback, what you hear at this stage will save your bacon a dozen ways before you go live and you end up with eggs all over your face.

Step Five: Build a few more profiles from the template

For me, this is the go/no go moment. Once you start building pages from the template, any change you make to the template will probably have to be made on existing content BY HAND. And as someone who once had to change 150 pages to reflect a change to the template, that's an easy way to lose a day.

So be 100% certain that the template is RIGHT.

Go back to your Google form and grab the rest of the completed forms and practice building new profiles from the survey results.

You might think about asking people who did a half-assed job on the first form to try again, but really, focus on getting 3-4 solid profiles right. They will serve as an example of what you're trying to do to people who aren't your cheerleaders.

Step Six: Push

Show the completed profiles to the people who write them and get their approval to share them. If you did your job right, they should be thrilled. But the last thing you want is for someone to freak out because they hate their photo or something. If you are using Wordpress, there is a plugin that allows you to share preview drafts with people before they go live. Share the previews in person if possible. Don't let them stew. Be in their faces as they look at the profile and get them to say, "I'm good with this." This will save you pain later.

Quietly push the new site live. Share the URL with your cheerleaders, your local leadership, and your recruiters. You might use an email that looks like this:

> In order to tell more of our authentic brand stories, the employer brand team has launched [Name of this site] at [URL].
>
> This is the first first step to tell dozens, if not hundreds of stories of the people who make this company great. We anticipate having a new round of profiles every week or two for the next three months and adjusting based on response.
>
> Please feel free to share a profile or the site on social media as this site works best as more people see it. If you're a recruiter, these might be the kinds of stories that attract more amazing candidates, so share them with prospects and people in your pipeline.
>
> If you have feedback, feel free to share it with me. But expect to see more profiles from every corner of the company in short order.
>
> Thanks for your support...

Unless someone from the C-suite comes down on you like a ton of bricks, keep going. Don't sweat the feedback (but listen to it). If you can see a future of hundreds of profiles and how you can use them to tell your story, just keep going.

Be smart and install Google Analytics on the site (it's free and easy). That will tell you how many people visit your new site, where they came from and how long the stay. This is great fodder for your metrics down the road (see how I'm looking out for you?).

Step Seven: Promote

If you've done this right, you should expect to see a few hundred visits to the site pretty quickly. You need to use that success to build more momentum internally and get more people to fill out your survey.

Pick ten more people you think might be potential cheerleaders and fans and send them an email like this:

> Hi!
>
> So I don't know if you've seen this, but we've launched a site to tell more of the staff's stories to the outside world. The goal is to shape candidates' perception of what its like to work here and attract more talent. Take a look at it here: [URL]
>
> I'm emailing because I really want to put you on the site. All it takes is fifteen minutes of your time to complete a survey and I'll take care of the rest. I'm not saying filling out the form is the path to becoming famous, but frankly, it can't hurt.
>
> I'd love for you to block off 15 minutes in your calendar in the next week and go to [LINK TO SURVEY]. Once you hit submit, I'll be in touch.
>
> Thanks so much in advance for your help. Let me know if you have questions.

Now, I'm going to let you in on a little secret. At some point, a manager will walk up beside you in line waiting for coffee or something and say, "You know, I saw that new site. It's great! If I had an employee I thought deserved recognition like that how would I make that happen?"

Yes, at some point, you'll stop having to beg for attention and people will start coming to you. In that case, I would ask for the employee's name and then send them this:

> Hi!
>
> Someone, possibly your boss, thinks you're pretty amazing and would like for you to show off a little.
>
> Please go to [LINK TO SURVEY] and complete as much of the form as you're comfortable. Eventually it will become a profile on [NAME OF SITE], which you can see at [URL].
>
> I am looking forward to making you a little famous. Let me know if you have any questions!

Step Eight: Tweak

At this stage, you're getting a nice volume of profile submissions. You might even be getting to the point where you are bulk-editing and bulk-uploading the content into the template and then scheduling each one to go out on its own day. Now that you've got a solid stream of content and this process isn't new anymore, it is time to tweak things.

Sure, you've probably been tweaking things here and there, but now you can pause a moment and think things through. Start by asking yourself these questions:

- What kind of traffic are you getting?
- Where are the biggest sources of traffic coming from? What pages are they hitting first?
- Is each post being shared by the subject?

- Do you want to push visitors to jobs or more content?
- What teams are well-represented and which need more representation?
- Are you getting much traffic to the category pages (profiles in a specific office or team)? If so, is it time to start spiffing them up with more content about the team/office at the top of the page before showing off the profiles?
- Is there a leader you should be targeting? Getting a C-suite person to complete the profile will show that this isn't "just for front-line staff."
- Are recruiters sharing the content? (We'll talk more about how to get recruiters to use this in a moment.)
- Is content being shared once, or semi-regularly?
- What pages are being landed on most, and what content should those pages have to be more useful to you?

If you want to connect your stories to related jobs, talk to your HRIS person who understands what your ATS can do. See if they can build URLs that link to job openings in specific offices or departments. You might not be able to connect a sales profile to a specific sales job (because at some point the requisition will close and the URL will break), but you might be able to connect it to a current listing of sales jobs.

Heck, if you're feeling wild and crazy, try and pull an RSS feed of specific team jobs and embed that listing into the template. That might be pretty advanced, but you should at least see what you can make happen.

Step Nine: Segment

This is the stage where we stop treating everyone equally.

If you're using Google Forms to collect data, you can use some simple logic to ask what team the person works in and then show a set of questions customized to that team. Maybe you'll want to ask developers if they prefer Emacs or Vim? Maybe you'll want to ask sales people about their biggest sales success.

Not only should you be segmenting the content coming in, you can segment how the content appears. Maybe you need to make a template specific for a specific team because they have great content and you really need to hire more of them.

Can you set up a way for people to upload short videos? It seems like everyone has a phone and or laptop with a camera, so take advantage of how the creative can tell their own stories their own way.

Heck, you could build a profile that is a standard article/blog post format to be scattered amongst the profiles. Perhaps you could connect with your tech teams or anyone else who occasionally publishes white papers or patents something. Threading this kind of content elevates and "proves" that the people you are profiling are doing amazing work.

Just start thinking about how to fine tune this content machine.

Step Ten: Manage

I'm not sure when this step happens, because it will probably feel like you've been "managing" this whole time, and you have. The difference is how do you manage content full time so that "getting it going" isn't your primary focus.

Things to consider at this stage:

Traffic numbers should be part of your metrics. So how do you increase traffic? Do you ask for your site to be mentioned by leadership at the next all-hands meeting? Do you work with the web team to link to your site from the central navigation? Do you link to the site from every single job posting? Are you maximizing the traffic social media can bring? What about alternative content sites like Quora or reddit?

One opportunity that might present itself at this stage is the chance to off-load day-to-day operations of the site onto someone else in your team. In fact, this could be a great opportunity for you to pitch adding some junior-level headcount to your team. They can manage the content and editing and you can focus more on strategy.

So if this section hasn't exhausted you (and it's no shame if it has a little), you might ask why is this in a book about working with recruiters? I'll give you a few good reasons.

One: Tell recruiter stories

At no point did I specifically say that you should build profiles for your recruiters, but you absolutely should. In fact, I'd recommend a few tweaks to their own pages.

Ask a question or two about what they look for in a great candidate. Also give them a chance to talk about their own recruiting process.

Then, find a way to link to requisitions they own (you'll almost certainly need to work with HRIS on this or on some kind of duct tape-like work around) from their page.

Include some basic contact information (LinkedIn, Email) so that a candidate can see how to contact the recruiter.

Finally, ask the recruiter to put a link to their profile pages in their email signature. This will help prospects and candidates feel a little more connected to the recruiter and keep the recruiter from looking like a faceless cog in an uncaring recruiting machine.

Two: They are going to use the content to engage prospects

You and I know that most recruiters seem to be a bunch of job requisition spewing monsters. They can't engage in a simple human conversation without asking "Want to join our team?" or "Would you be willing to apply?"

Okay, that's true. But to the candidate it probably sounds about right. When was the last time a recruiter reached out to you and didn't immediately pitch a job opening to you? Probably rarely, if ever. Which is why most people have some pretty strong shields designed to deflect such obvious outreach.

But what if, instead of sending a link to a job posting, they sent something interesting? What if they sent you a profile about someone in their company who did a similar job as you with the note that said, "in case you wondered how other companies get it done..."

Suddenly, the recruiter isn't one of those salespeople in a quiet store who seems dead set on selling you something. They become useful purveyors of interesting stories. If you're good at what you do, you are probably interested in seeing how others do it. And if you read the story and think, "wow, that sounds like a great way to do it. I wonder if they're hiring..." isn't the recruiter infinitely better positioned? And won't they get a better outreach response?

Three: This is how they start building relationships
Most recruiters are very transactionally-focused. They are there to fill roles and put butts in seats. It's the way most recruiters have worked since the advent of the rolodex. But it's not the only way to recruit. In fact, a lot of companies are moving to a more relationship-driven recruiting, where prospects are kept warm until the

right opens up. It tends to lower costs and shorten time to fill, but it is still a fairly new idea for recruiters, mostly because recruiters are equipped to be relationship-focused.

But your content can change all that. By feeding them profiles like this on a regular basis (and in the section, we'll get more into the "how"), they can build connections with people they aren't going to hire. If all you have is a job opening to share, the only person you'll attract are those people looking for jobs. If you share content, you'll connect with smart people you can tap down the road.

So you might need to sell this concept to recruiters, showing them how sending a profile of the right person sparks conversation and engagement and keeps them from being yet another sales person. It will take a little time to get them to come around and make content sharing part of their regular workday, but they can't get there until the content is available first.

YOUR WEEKLY EMPLOYER BRAND NEWSLETTER

You might start noting a trend here: you get recruiters to do what you want by doing as much of the work for them as possible. Good eye!

Now that you've got all this amazing content coming in at a steady clip, how do you make sure your recruiters are using it? By wrapping it up in a pretty little bow and delivering it regularly.

I suggest that you start a weekly "Employer Brand Update" newsletter and subscribe all your recruiters and cheerleaders to it. In that newsletter, you'll share your (useful!) team updates, any new content coming out, but also 1-3 three prepared and packaged pieces of content you'd like everyone to share on social.

Here's what to do:

Step One: Pick a Platform
There are a number of email newsletter platforms

out there, and some are free. You also have an internal email program you use all the time for work. You need to pick a platform on which to build your newsletter. There are pros and cons for each.

Professional email platforms are designed to help people who pay a lot of money send a lot of email to a lot of people. They often have very complex analytics tool and content development tools to help massive companies get the most out of their daily newsletters. This is almost certainly overkill for what you are going to do. But platforms like Tinyletter and Mailchimp offer free versions for smaller users like you that let you build the skill of mass-sending emails even if you only have a dozen recipients. There are two major "pros" for these platforms. First, they can send gorgeous emails. But of course, these companies have staffs of people there to make graphics for the emails. You might not have that. But they also have features that allow strangers to subscribe to your newsletter without your involvement. So if a hiring manager wanted to subscribe, they could, just like you were the nichiest and nerdiest version of The Skimm.

Work-based email platforms (Outlook, Gmail, et al) are much easier to use. In fact, you're probably already an expert. These won't offer automatic subscription tools, but they may offer some simple templates and a way to create a listserv-like mailing list within the program. You'll have to manage the list by hand, but that's not going to be a huge volume, is it? The real bonus is that because you're a known user on the email server, your emails won't be flagged as spam.

Obviously, I suggest you start on a local platform, and if this becomes wildly successful, migrate to something bigger.

Step Two: Build a Content Structure

So every week, you're going to send content. Like the content machine, build a plan for what kind of content you expect to push out and design a template around it. For example, you might build a structure like this:

- Headline (in nice big letters that provide a smidge of branding, maybe even as an image header)
- Updates (new platforms launched, new campaigns to look out for, legitimate successes to announce, etc. These are in blurb-format)
- Featured content (1-3 profiles you've selected because of other things happening on calendar or just because you want to promote them)
  - If you really want people to share them, make it easy: write up the actual tweet above the link to the profile. That way people just have to copy the text and URL and drop it into Twitter, Facebook or LinkedIn.
  - See more details in the "social media content" section
- Other new content (bullets of profiles and stories that are brand new even if you aren't promoting them yet so recruiters know what new profiles and related roles they have access to)

Step Three: Subscribe People

This one is easy. Research how to make a distribution list on your platform and add in every recruiter in your company. Then add in any and all TA and HR leadership and any cheerleaders who've been helpful in the past.

Make sure to put a line at the end of your emails that say if someone wants to be subscribed, just reply to the email (which is being sent directly by you). Also list that if someone wants to be removed from the list, to just ask.

Step Four: Build the Habit

The easiest way to build the habit is to book the habit. Go into your calendar and block off an hour one or twice a week to focus on writing up the newsletter. There's just no other way to ensure that the work gets done consistently. In fact, this also sets the expectation from readers that your newsletter will come at roughly the same day and time every time, building its own credibility internally.

Let recruiters get used to getting it. Every once in a while, take a look at recruiter's LinkedIn feeds and see who is using the content and who isn't. Talk to the people who are using it and ask them to talk up the value of posting the content and how it helps them fill their pipeline and build connections rather than try and cajole recruiters into doing something they don't want to do. If you can get the recruiters who are using your content to mention how it has helped them close a specific requisition quickly (and thus lower their overall time to fill scores), that tends to really encourage your laggards into trying something new.

RECRUITER'S TOOLKIT

An alternative to the weekly newsletter is to build and actively maintain a recruiter's toolkit. It won't solve the problem of delivering regular content to the recruiters to share, but it will establish a great baseline to get them started.

Think of it less as a source of content, but as a touchstone to what you need all recruiters (and potentially hiring managers) to understand about your employer brand and how they can help present it to the world. This is a set of shared instructions on what your expectations are from recruiting, and how it will help them.

The first step is to figure out where it should live. Your first instinct might be to put it on the company intranet, but I have yet to meet a company or staff member who actually liked their intranet. Commonly, they become the collective junk drawer of the company, the place where manuals, policy guides, well-meaning news feeds and other detritus collect like so many old chopsticks, bits of string and keys whose purpose has long been forgotten.

That's not the fate you want for your toolkit, is it? Of course not. So be sure that's where it has to go before you accept it as the default position. Because there might be a better option. You could make it public.

It's not as crazy an idea as it might seem at first blush. First, you want this content to be easily findable. Second, none of this content is a secret. You want people to share it widely, don't you? Isn't that the purpose of your brand? There's not too much downside to having it live, other than you'll have to double check everything you upload. That's not much cost.

Once you have a landing spot for it, you can decide what to put on it.

First, the page should serve as a reminder of what you want recruiters to do: tell your brand story. So make it easy. There's value in writing a version of that story for everyone, as it will get people sharing faster. Over time, you might consider trimming it back once everyone understands what they need to be communicating and you want to encourage recruiters and other staff to tell their own version of that story. The more you put words in their mouth, the less room there is for their own words. But to get the ball rolling, it makes sense to feed them some lines.

Next, what is some evergreen content you want them to share. Not "flavor of the week" stuff but videos and stories that have a far longer halflife. Add metadata suggesting what messages each piece of content conveys and some instances where it would be useful to share it.

You can and should add in everything from hashtag suggestions, training on LinkedIn profile development, where resources for content and collateral are stored, and content information. This is the sort of thing where you can put a lot of stuff, but you need to think through why the content is there and make it as easy for even the most skeptical recruiter as possible.

By way of example, I am in love with what Foundation Medicine did (full disclosure, it was built by Audra Knight, who is a friend of mine, but please don't hold that against her). Google "foundation medicine talent brand toolkit" and it should pop right up. It is an amazing example of how you can support your recruiters and align them to your strategy without feeling overwhelming or demanding.

SOCIAL MEDIA CONTENT

What passes for "social media recruiting content" these days is really quite sad. Over and over, I see LinkedIn posts by recruiters that simply say, "Apply now!" or "We're hiring!" or "Join me!" These YARPs (Yet Another Recruiting Post) are wastes of space, not only because they say nothing meaningful, not only because they take up the space where meaningful content might be found, not only because they don't differentiate the recruiter, job or company at all, but because their use lets other people think saying this is okay. It allows such deep mediocrity to continue.

I have some feelings here, clearly.

So if you've made a content machine and want recruiters to share these lovely jewels you've built for them, you probably need to teach them how to share them on social media properly. Rather than send them to social media bootcamp (though, that wouldn't be the worst idea I've ever heard), let's focus on a few small changes in thinking that will yield huge benefits.

First rule: Only job seekers want to see job postings (and they already know where to find them). I get that to a recruiter, job postings are the coin of the realm. So it's totally understandable that they think their job is to distribute and propagate those postings everywhere they can. But that's a very 1980's way of thinking, where jobs were mostly clustered in the Sunday papers, so getting early word of a new opening might have been useful. These days, people looking for jobs already know where to look. Telling people not looking for a job about a job is like wandering around the mall parking lot offering to sell someone a car - I mean, there might be someone who happens to have the time and money in pocket to take advantage, but if they were really looking, they know where the car lot is, thanks.

So the focus of all recruiter social media content should be stories rather than jobs.

Stories are just universally interesting. Unless you're in the middle of surgery or putting a fire out, an interesting story is worth stopping for and hearing. They appeal to almost anyone, but can be focused to specific audiences.

Stories have the added advantage of not needing an immediate call to action. They can simply be engaging and create a little positive brand awareness. That positive brand awareness pays off when they search for a job one day and the job board returns hundreds of openings. You want them to see your logo and think, "oh yeah, they were pretty interesting" and click it open. Or maybe the person decides to connect with the recruiter because of the story. That extends the recruiter's network with almost no work at all.

Finally, as the recruiter focuses on the audiences they serve (nurses, product marketers, accountants, etc), sharing stories about those people establishes their credibility to those audiences. If a recruiter of accountants is posting accounting and finance articles to accountant forums and groups, they will build a reputation as someone who really "gets" accountants. They become a resource for accountants. So when an accountant wants to look for a job, who do you think they will engage first? The recruiter who has shown a willingness to engage on the accountants' own turf.

Second rule: The purpose is to get someone to click. Now, as you share your new stories with recruiting, you should write up what the text around the link should be. Aside from making the post more attractive, you'll be training recruiters what's acceptable and what's not. It is easy, When writing up a post, the fastest way to write it is to summarize the content. What's it about? It's about this.

The problem is that if you've summarized the content in the tweet or the LinkedIn post, why would they click the link to read it in a longer format?

The goal of good social media writing is to entice, not explain. In fact, you are probably going to lean on the four drivers of social media reading: Entertain, Inspire, Educate, Inform. So ensure that social content gets the job done, you want to train your recruiters to think about which of the four drivers the content will deliver and make the social post about the driver.

For example, if the story is about someone who runs a dog shelter, it is ripe for being an inspirational story. Rather than write the post about the dogs or the shelter, write the post about how the story might inspire you to see the animals around you differently.

If the story is about a new way to code, that sounds like an education post. So don't write about the code, but about how learning about the code will help you develop better programs.

If you make the four drivers clear to recruiters and make sure every post you share in the newsletter reflects that, you'll teach them to write better overall.

There's one more trick I'd like to share that you can pass along to select recruiters. For recruiters who have mastered the four drivers, there is a next level. Google "Sumo Headline Formulas" and take a look at what Sumo has put together. When I first found this site years ago, it was 48 formulas, but they've since come up with a few more, so it really is a live training document you should be leveraging.

The formulas are based on everything from click-bait headlines, email subject lines which got great response and other marketing psychology experiments. What I love about these is that it shows the formula and how to apply it. It may seem like a lot at first, but most people tend to gravitate to a handful of the formulas and ignore the rest.

Bonus: use these same headline formulas to write better headlines for your job postings.

METRICS

I both love and hate metrics when it comes to employer branding. On one hand, I love seeing the outcome of doing good work, or seeing where my strategy hasn't connected like I'd hoped so I can make changes.

But metrics are dangerous. When it comes to a weird and strange role like employer brand, it becomes very easy and absolutely tragic when the metrics drive action. If you have a 3.5 Glassdoor strategy and you figure out ways to game the system to bring the number up to a 4.5 with making your company obviously better to work for, you haven't managed your brand, you've white washed a ratings site.

I don't want that job.

But metrics show improvement and underscore value, something crucial to your ability to get meetings with influencers within the company and make the desired impact. So you need to cherry pick what metrics you watch and which you share.

Metrics You Watch
- Social media engagement numbers (to learn what people are responding to and what isn't working)
- Social media reach numbers (no one cares how many followers you have on LinkedIn and Facebook because you'll still have to pay money to reach them all)
- Hashtag usage (if you have one, just to see how it is being implemented)
- Pipeline metrics (numbers of candidates who apply, number screened, to understand changes in volume)
- Rough percentage of job postings that use your model (so you understand where work still needs to be done)

Metrics You Share
- Traffic to your content (to show the impact of your content and how many people it reaches)
- Time to fill (to show that content that creates relationships shortens TTF)
- Referral rate (to show that
- Traffic from social (to show that changing how everyone thinks about
- Traffic from campaigns (if applicable, to show that your marketing thinking is driving in eyeballs)
- Glassdoor and other rating sites (to show broad sentiment)
- Offer conversion rate (this is to help reinforce that your job is never really done)

I would guess you'll be sharing a report with your leadership at least every month, but make a stripped down version just for recruiters to show that you are doing your part and how your work is impacting their work.

EMAIL SIGNATURES

This might not apply at your company, but email signatures are one of those things that people don't give much thought to or of how many people see them. And if we're talking about recruiters, people who are effectively professional email senders, their signature could probably be doing more.

Now, if your company already has an agreed-upon look and feel for your email signature, and the team that owns that signature is… less flexible than you'd like (it isn't a dig at them, because I understand where they are coming from), you either have to start lobbying slowly for an alternative signature for recruiting, pull a full guerilla marketing campaign and go around them, or just let the idea go. You'll have to make that call.

But the goal here isn't to make some sort of complicated and complex layout that dominates all but the most wordy emails. It is to help establish and reinforce your employer brand positioning, and to provide a clear and simple call to action to people who might be ready for it.

If your recruiter has a profile page completed including what they tend to recruit for and how they like to work, that's probably the best thing to point people to. How you word your call to action and the link is what will reinforce your brand position. For example, here are some broad brand positions and possible CTAs to the profile page:

Brand Position	Email CTA to Recruiter Profile
Prestige	I'm a little bit famous. Check it out!
Opportunity	Take a look at the people who are building [COMPANY], like me!
Support / Team	I am just one of the many people who love working together at [COMPANY]
Stability	I am X years into my tenure at [COMPANY]. What are you looking for?
Innovation	Meeting the people creating the future, like me!

If you don't have recruiter pages up just yet, you can either point them to the career site or your site of profiles (if it's different). Again, make sure your working supports the overall brand positioning you're cultivating.

AFTERWORD

I know something about you. You're crazy.

You know how I know? Because the kind of person who is told that a role involves being partially responsible for every aspect of a company but has no direct authority to make change and says, "Yeah, I'll take that job!" is stone cold crazy.

Don't worry. Everyone in employer branding is nuttier than a cast reunion of Tiger King. Except with fewer big cats and slightly nerdier conversations.

Learning that your brand of insanity is not completely unique, that you aren't alone in your madness, is often helpful. That knowledge has certainly helped me.

So if you get stuck, if you need help, find your local community of employer branders, be it on Facebook, LinkedIn, Whatsapp or Twitter, and ask for help.

Because along with being crazy, employer branders are also strangely nice and willing to share.

Don't do it alone. You'll be more successful and maybe even a little happier because of it.

-James "Employer Brand Nerd" Ellis, April 16, 2020

YOU WANT MORE?

Oh, I have more.

First, sign up for my weekly newsletter for fellow employer brand practitioners. It is a digest of the conversations around the industry and peeks outside the industry to help keep you sharp as things evolve. Go to employerbrand.news to sign up.

Next, I have a podcast. I know! So does everyone else! But mine is different in that it is now in its fourth year of production. It's not a bunch of interviews (though I do occasionally bring in my friends because they are insanely smart), or places for PR folks to plant softball puff pieces. It is a weekly deep dive into higher-order thinking around every possible aspect of employer branding. It's called The Talent Cast and it's available wherever you get podcasts, or from thetalentcast.com.

Finally, if you want me to come talk about employer

brand thinking at your event or webinar, email me! I'd love to find a way to help! I'm at jamesoellis@gmail. com, or find me on LinkedIn at http://linkedin.com/in/ thewarfortalent.

ABOUT JAMES ELLIS

Before falling in love with the art and craft of employer branding, James Ellis was a digital marketer with 15 years experience in how audiences think and behave online. Since then, he has taken those skills to become one of employer branding's leading voices and practitioners.

In his career, James has worked with dozens of brands from companies of every size and shape like Disney, Target, Tradeshift, CNH Industrial, Regeneron, Enova, QuEST Global, and many others. As an in-house practitioner, he transformed Groupon's employer brand, reaching Hired's list of strongest employer brands in Chicago after spending a stunningly small amount of budget.

James' mission is to evolve the conversation around recruiting and hiring. In order to serve that mission to the widest possible audience and make that evolution accessible to any recruiter or marketer, he has hosted

The Talent Cast podcast for more than three years, hosted the Employer Brand Headlines newsletter and written for a number of industry publications like RecruitingDaily, ERE, Indeed Blog, Recruitment Marketing Magazine, Talent Economy, The Chad and Cheese podcast, Marketing People podcast, Strong Suit podcast, and the Recruiting Future podcast. He has spoken at SHRM, MRA, Hired's Roadshow, HireConf, Social Recruiting Strategies Conference, RecruitCon, and to multiple private clients. He was also an inaugural member of the Talent Brand Alliance board.

He lives in Chicago with his wife and daughter. You can find him on Twitter @TheWarForTalent, EmployerBrand.News, TheTalentCast.com or just LinkedIn (duh). And yes, he would love another cup of coffee, thank you.

###

Printed in Great Britain
by Amazon

16526091R00071